HOW TO BEAT BULLYING AT SCHOOL

Simple steps to put an end to bullying

Written by Marie Léon
Translated by Ciaran Traynor

Health and Wellbeing   50MINUTES.com

Should I make my child move school to spare them further pain?

What should I do if my child is the one who is doing the bullying?

As a teacher, how can I bring up bullying in class?

FURTHER READING   26

HOW TO BEAT BULLYING AT SCHOOL

- **Problem**: repeated violence, baiting, insults, being left out... Bullying has terrible consequences for victims. Although this problem was glossed over in the past, anti-bullying campaigns have now been implemented in schools. The issue is now being addressed more and more. However, parents and teachers too often find themselves helpless against this scourge.
- **Aims**: to understand bullying and to help your child confront it and fight it with the tools they have at their disposal.
- **FAQs**:
  - Can all children be victims of bullying?
  - I think that my child was beaten up at school. Will they talk to me about it?
  - How can I tell if my child is being bullied?
  - What should I do if my child is being bullied?
  - Should I make my child move school to spare them further pain?
  - What should I do if my child is the one who is doing the bullying?
  - As a teacher, how can I bring up bullying in class?

Although bullying in schools is not a recent phenomenon, it has only begun to gain public attention over the last few years. It is fortunate that bullying is now being treated seriously: according to the Annual Bullying Survey 2016, 1.5 million young people in the UK are victims of bullying every year. This figure is all the more frightening because of the significant damage bullying causes: loss of self-confidence, problems at school leading to young people dropping out, psychological consequences, suicide attempts, and more...

For an act to be considered bullying, it has to recur, intend to harm and lead to a dominant-dominated situation. Bullying therefore does not include fights and other arguments which children can sometimes be involved in during their time at school. It is more likely to take the form of insults, mockery, degrading nicknames, hitting, and rumours spread to damage their reputation, which the victim may have to face every day.

Although this scourge was limited to school grounds in the past, nowadays it is much more invasive because it has spread to social media. As a result, the victim never has a moment's peace. Moreover, this problem also leads to an insidious deterioration of the atmosphere in the school. Due to the extent of this problem, organisations such as BullyingUK and the Anti-Bullying Alliance have been set up to take a stand against bullying, and the Anti-Bullying Week is now organised every year to raise awareness about this serious problem.

When faced with the distress the victim can find themselves in, it is particularly difficult to find the words to help them. That is why this guide will give you some tools and tips so you have the best chance of beating this common problem.

WHAT IS BULLYING?

ACTS OF VIOLENCE WITH TRAGIC CONSEQUENCES

According to recent statistics, around 50% of children suffer from bullying in the UK. The perpetrator of this violence may be acting alone or they may be at the head of a small group which they turn against one child in particular. They therefore create an imbalance of power between themselves and their victim, who they bully on a daily basis over a relatively long period of time, to the point of making them into a scapegoat. Although the most visible acts of violence are physical (fighting, hitting, damaging personal belongings, etc.), they are often accompanied by verbal (ridicule, insults, mocking, etc.) and psychological (blackmail, isolation, rumours, etc.) violence, which is more insidious and difficult to detect. This kind of abuse frequently escapes adult attention, because more often than not it takes place during break or outside of school.

DID YOU KNOW?

Many of the children who took part in recent anti-bullying campaigns had suffered physical injuries such as bruises, and some had even had their fingers jammed in vices or their belongings stolen or damaged. What is more, many reported being the subject of insinuations, sniggering and comments during school trips, and some girls were even the subject of rumours that they

Victims of bullying have the impression of being very alone, and they sometimes even feel a deep sense of isolation and helplessness. They are often smaller or weaker than their tormentors and are therefore incapable of defending themselves. Most of the time, since the tormentors begin to harass them even more as the time passes, fear and insecurity set in, as well as a feeling of powerlessness and even guilt.

> "I was bullied when I was a child, more than 20 years ago. It was really hell, and it went on for months. Unfortunately, at the time, there were none of the anti-bullying organisations that exist now. I eventually found the courage to go to see one of my teachers, who helped me a lot. I felt guilty even though I was the victim." (Paul, 40)

Children who are made to suffer this abuse and bullying go through hell every day. Their feeling of misery grows with every week, or even every month – and sometimes even every year! – that their torture continues. As soon as Sunday night comes, the anxiety about returning to school gets stronger and stronger, and they go off to school every morning in the clutches of fear. However, apart from at breakfast, when children sometimes have trouble eating, bullied children and teenagers are often incredibly inventive when it comes to pretending that everything is fine. However, there are still some signs which can make parents aware that everything is not as it should be: recurring headaches, imaginary illnesses, invented pretexts to stay off school, uncharacteristic aggressiveness, sleeping problems, loss of appetite, and so on.

When the bullying continues and the child is not supported by their classmates, they become completely isolated: they have no close friends – in fact, they have no friends at all – and their universe is reduced to them and nothing else. This feeling, added to the violence which they are made to suffer, leads to a terrible kind of suffering which can even result in suicidal thoughts.

WHY ARE SOME CHILDREN REJECTED?

Bullying arises primarily from the simple refusal of difference. This rejection leads to the stigmatisation of some of the victim's characteristics. It generally takes place in primary school or in secondary school. Depending on the age of those involved, it can be due to the way the victim dresses, possibly more modestly or less fashionably, or even a body type which does not fit the norm. This distinctive characteristic becomes an ideal target for ridicule: children can be attacked for having a big nose, ears that stick out, freckles, being overweight, and so on. It does not take long before nasty nicknames appear, which are the first sign that a child is being excluded from the group. Besides physical appearance, children can also be isolated if their academic results are too good or if their family is not like most others (same-sex parents, an absent mother or father, etc.).

> "Everything began when I changed primary school. I moved to a hard school, with a lot of rebellious children. I was by far the best student and they didn't like that at all. I was made to suffer every torture imaginable: I was hit, given nicknames, insulted, and my bag was even opened and all of my things thrown into the dirt. I couldn't tell anyone about it, I was ashamed, I thought that it was all my fault. Eventually, I stopped working in class so they would leave me alone. I ended up having to repeat the year but, thankfully, I also changed school. It's taken me years to be able to talk about this terrible period in my life." (Sophia, 30)

HOW CAN YOU BE SURE THAT A CHILD IS BEING BULLIED?

Behaviour is defined as bullying when it meets several of the criteria below:

- a number of repeated repeated physical, verbal and psychological attacks;
- acts of violence which continue over a long period of time and are always committed by the same student or students;
- an aggressor-victim relationship where one party dominates and the other submits;
- a growing fear in the victim.

IS BULLYING A GROUP PHENOMENON?

In all bullying cases, there are never just two parties involved, but three: the victim, the bully and the witnesses.
At first, the bully is alone and their attention is drawn to
a classmate they do not like. Their victim is generally more
fragile and vulnerable, and the tormentor quickly realises
that the child they do not like is afraid of them and cannot
defend themselves. The bully therefore goes on the attack.
When other students see that there are no consequences
for the bully, they decide to join them, in order to gain the
favour of the 'leader', or even to protect themselves against
possible bullying.

On the edge of this group are the witnesses, those who
observe from afar in silence. They are aware of what is going
on, but they do not have the courage to intervene, because
that would inevitably lead to retaliation and they would
then find themselves the victims of the bully. They therefore
prefer to turn a blind eye.

CYBERBULLYING: A NEW KIND OF BULLYING

Over the last few years, blogs, email, social networks
and mobile phones have made victims' lives even more
excruciating, because their torture is no longer confined to
school. This new form of bullying, known as cyberbullying,
is worrying due to the extent of the damage it can cause,
because the anonymity of the internet and the possibility of
being able to use a different name gives the tormentor the
impression that they can do what they want without being

punished.

Its power also comes from the fact that children are beginning to use these tools from a younger and younger age. Nowadays, it is not unusual to find primary schools where pupils constantly use their phones. During class, the majority of teachers ask students to turn off their phones but, once they are in the playground, pupils just turn them back on again. Nowadays, it could not be easier to send an insulting text to someone, write something nasty online, or spread photos, both compromising ones and ones which just aim to mock. It is not long before this information becomes the talk of the school, and it can even go further than that, because anyone with access to the internet can find it. With tools like these, bullying becomes constant, and psychological suffering increases dramatically.

HOW TO FIGHT BULLYING

HOW CAN I TELL IF I'M BEING BULLIED?

Recently at school, for no apparent reason:

- your classmates make fun of you;
- they damage your things, your books, and sometimes even your clothes;
- they steal your mobile phone, your money or your snack;
- they give you nasty nicknames based on your appearance or your family;
- they laugh when you take part in class;
- they constantly push you to antagonise you;
- you feel isolated and are forced to play and eat alone...

Unfortunately, if some of these descriptions apply to you, then you are being bullied. The consequences for your future can be terrible if you do not react, in terms of both your education (you may drop out) and your health (physically, if there is violence involved, and psychologically, because of the deep sense of unhappiness that you feel). The first thing to do is therefore to come to terms with the fact that the situation you are in is not normal and cannot be accepted: you do not need to suffer ridicule or violence from your classmates. Moreover, you are not in the slightest bit responsible for what has happened to you, but you cannot keep it to yourself: speak to a parent, a teacher you trust or even an organisation, because they can find solutions to put an end to your problem. You will need a lot of courage to escape your solitude, but you can do it.

By discussing what is going on at school with people who you trust, you will see that you are not alone and that other children are also being bullied by a classmate. Do not be afraid to visit the websites of companies who fight against bullying (such as the Anti-Bullying Alliance site) or to phone an anti-bullying hotline so you can talk about what has happened to you without giving your identity (you can reach the National Bullying Helpline on 0845 22 55 787 or 07734 701221)

AS A TEACHER, WHAT SHOULD I DO IF I SUSPECT THAT A CHILD IS BEING BULLIED?

It is often difficult for teachers to know if there really is any bullying going on or not, because it often takes place far from adult eyes. However, there are certain signs which should put you on your guard, such as marks left by physical attacks, theft and isolation. If you realise that something is going on, make sure you keep a record of how often it occurs and if it is a long-term problem.

If a child comes to you to ask for help, the most important thing to do is to listen to them. If you have to ask questions, make sure they are very open and be careful to never take sides. The next thing to do is to explain what will be done to solve the problem.

Once the victim tells you about their problems, you should discuss them with your colleagues and the headteacher to decide on a course of action. When you speak with the bully, you should encourage them to recognise the impact of what they have done on the victim, without ever revealing their name.

Anti-bullying organisations also suggest that schools should run anti-bullying campaigns in order to make students aware of this problem. You can organise lessons focusing on bullying, during which anti-bullying videos made by children can be shown to older students and cartoons to the younger ones, and finish with a debate between students. On the Anti-Bullying Campaign site there are over 100 tools for teachers to use to combat bullying and raise awareness among students.

HOW CAN I TELL IF MY CHILD IS BEING BULLIED?

Even if a bullied child does everything they can to keep it a secret, out of fear of what will happen if their classmates find out that they have complained or told on the bullies, there are still several warning signs which can reveal what is going on:

- your child does not want to go to school anymore;
- they constantly complain of stomach aches, headaches or even imaginary illnesses;
- they feel nauseous and throw up;
- they ask you to take them to school or, on the contrary, categorically refuse that you come with them;
- they no longer want to play sports with their classmates;
- they stop seeing their friends;
- they suddenly have marks of physical violence on their

body or their face, such as scratches or bruises;
- they come home with torn clothes;
- their supplies have been damaged or vanished;
- they ask you for more pocket money than usual;
- they seem to be more tired;
- they do not do their homework and their grades are suffering;
- they avoid talking with you;
- they lose their appetite;
- they suddenly shut themselves away in their room for no reason;
- they seem more intolerant and more temperamental, and sometimes even aggressive.

Unfortunately, this list is far from exhaustive, but if you notice that your child displays several of these signs, especially if they recur, then it is possible that they are being bullied.

You should also watch how your child behaves with their brothers and sisters, particularly if they are younger. Some children who are bullied at school become more aggressive at home, when they are in their comfort zone.

HOW CAN I BROACH THE SUBJECT WITH MY CHILD?

Victims of bullying can often feel guilty and believe they are responsible. They might also fear that they will not be believed if the situation is serious, and therefore prefer to keep quiet. Or they might simply be afraid of what might happen to them if the bullies are punished. Their self-image is also damaged: they lose their self-confidence and believe that others are not interested in them, which may lead them to think that their parents do not think highly of them either.

If you feel that your child is ready to talk to you, you could, for example, make a general statement in order to start the conversation: "I get the feeling that things aren't great at school at the moment. Are you sure that everything's ok?" If they seem to want to confide in you, speak to them calmly by listing all the things you have noticed in their behaviour, without ever judging them.

Bruno Humbeeck is a psycho-paediatrician who advises parents to reassure their child both of the fact that they are not alone and that there are other children with the same problems, and of the fact that a solution will be found. You should also encourage them not to be ashamed to talk about it, either with you, their friends or an organisation. Moreover, explain to them that they should not accept being dominated. This is obviously a difficult task for a child, which will take a long time to accomplish, but you can help them to see it through. You should also let them know that you are there to listen to and help them.

At first, they might dig their heels in, refuse to answer you, become aggressive or begin to cry. If it is clear that the conversation is going nowhere, suggest that they talk to someone else. Sometimes children can consider asking adults for help to be humiliating. You therefore have to be very patient and make them understand that you are there for them. You can also casually mention the names of anti-bullying websites. The impression that they are being listened to should also reassure them a little.

It is often advisable to take your child to a psychologist, who can support the two of you in your journey of acceptance and recovery, by giving you advice in order to get back to a normal life.

WHAT IS THE NEXT STEP?

Meet teachers

Since school is the source of all your child's problems, do not be afraid to set up a confidential meeting with the staff after speaking to your child. Meet with the senior staff and explain to them what your child is suffering on a daily basis. Make sure you set out the problems they are facing clearly and concretely. In order to do so, draw up a precise list of what you have noticed and the moment when everything began, in your opinion. The aim is to make the teachers aware of what is going on, so they can watch how the children interact in class and in the playground, and to allow them to collectively come up with solutions to protect your child. Depending on the situation, the bully might be suspended or even expelled after making them aware of the repercussions of their actions.

If your child is being humiliated by a member of the teaching staff, set up a meeting with them to discuss it, as calmly as possible. It is quite possible that the teacher did not mean any harm, and was just exasperated by a child who was slower than the others or had a self-satisfied attitude. However, if the teacher really did mean to harm or was even being genuinely cruel, you should talk to the headteacher. That being said, it can be very difficult to get incompetent teachers punished for their actions.

School nurses often see students of all ages and could therefore help you in your search for answers, as could the education counsellor or even the social worker. You could also ask a member of the Parent Council to assist you in your task.

Make a complaint

Bullying is punishable by the law, even if the act has not been committed on the school premises. If you think it will help, you or your child can make a complaint. However, be aware that these procedures often take a long time.

If the bully is punished, their parents may be instructed to compensate the victim's parents. Moreover, if the bully is over the age of ten and their actions are serious enough, they run the risk of a fine or even imprisonment in a Secure Children's Home, a Secure Training Centre of a Young Offender Institution. They might also be sentenced to community service to make them take responsibility for their actions. Aggravating circumstances, such as bullying a disabled child, can worsen the punishment.

If your child wishes to make a complaint themselves, there is no need for an adult to be there: in the UK, anyone can lodge a complaint about bullying.

WHERE CAN I GET HELP?

In the UK, there are two main anti-bullying numbers you can call: 0845 22 55 787 and 07734 701221. They are run by the National Bullying Helpline, which is available from 9am to 5pm Monday to Saturday, although urgent calls will also be taken after hours. You can also reach Childline at 0800 1111, which, although it does not specialise in bullying, is available to anyone in the UK under 19 and can be called at any time.

There are also several sites which may be helpful:

- BullyingUK, a part of the Family Lives website, covers a range of topics relating to bullying, including advice for parents, schools and young people. It deals with many of the situations that can arise from bullying and gives suggestions of where you can go for help. It also explains some of the anti-bullying campaigns which run in the UK, such as Anti-Bullying Week, which normally takes place at some point during November.
- NOBullying.com is an online forum which aims to raise awareness of and consequently stop bullying. The website began as a way to educate people about bullying, as there was little up-to-date, reliable information and advice about the problem online. It focuses particularly on cyberbullying, but it also has a range of articles on a variety of bullying-related topics.

HOW TO HELP YOUR CHILD TO RECOVER FROM BULLYING

REMIND THEM THAT THEY ARE NOT ALONE

In 2004, the first Anti-Bullying Week ran from 22 to 26 November. This event also saw the launch of the "Stand up for us" policy, which aims to combat homophobia in UK schools. Anti-Bullying Week, which has now become an annual event, allows victims of bullying to find a glimmer of hope after what they have gone through. It raises awareness of bullying, the problems associated with it and where victims can go to for help, and it can be a great relief for children to realise that there are people who can help them. Sometimes, that is all that is needed to break the cycle.

This kind of event is crucial to draw public attention to a problem which is affecting more and more pupils, and it is also important in raising awareness about the role that everyone has to play in order to stamp out this scourge once and for all. As a result, bullying is beginning to be recognised as a serious threat to young people's health and wellbeing, and various laws and debates have since been introduced to combat it; cyberbullying was even debated in parliament in 2013.

Once your child tells you about the torture they are being made to suffer at school, you must make sure you are always there for them so they feel supported and, more importantly, believed. However, overprotecting them is the last thing you should do, because this could make them more afraid and uncertain.

HELP THEM TO REDISCOVER THEIR JOY FOR LIFE

After taking action and helping them to get out of the hell they were going through, parents have to think about their child's future. They have to show them that school does not reflect life as a whole, that they are loved (and not only by their parents) and that they matter.

A good way to take their mind off bullying is for them to find an extracurricular activity with the help of their parents: a sport; a youth group; or piano, art or theatre classes. It does not really matter which activity you choose; the most important thing is to find something that they like and which will allow them to meet different people, so that they can see that not everyone is violent and contemptuous, and that they too deserve to have friends.

If they want to, going to see a psychologist can also do a child good. In fact, it is even strongly advised if the bullying has been going on for more than a year. Indeed, if the child is incapable of accepting and dealing with what they have gone through in a healthy manner, this can have an extremely damaging effect on their adult life.

Finally, even if the bullying began on social media, there is no point in taking their internet access away from them. You need to strike a balance so they do not feel isolated, or even excluded, once again. However, do not be afraid to lay out specific rules for the internet and change the connection settings on all of their devices with internet access.

CAN ALL CHILDREN BE VICTIMS OF BULLYING?

Bullying mostly affects children who are particularly sensitive or timid, or those who are a bit different: for example, a girl seen to be too masculine, an effeminate boy, a child with a physical abnormality or a brilliant student. Whatever their nature, differences can cause other students to reject children, as they may be conformist or jealous of this quality or trait which they do not have. Children who are easily influenced or vulnerable are obviously the preferred targets of these tormentors, who can sense that their victims will not defend themselves.

I THINK THAT MY CHILD WAS BEATEN UP AT SCHOOL. WILL THEY TALK TO ME ABOUT IT?

Not necessarily, because children often prefer to keep bullying a secret, out of fear of the repercussions or because of shame and guilt. Moreover, they will probably not want to share this problem with their parents, but would prefer to talk about it with children their own age or, better yet, with associations where they will be completely anonymous.

The fear of not being taken seriously or not being believed can also make bullied children think twice before talking about their problem with their family. However, if their self-confidence is still relatively intact and you have a good relationship founded on trust, they might decide to talk to you about the hell they are going through.

If you feel that they do not want to open up to you, do not push them. They might withdraw into themselves. Give them the names of associations where they will be able to express themselves freely.

HOW CAN I TELL IF MY CHILD IS BEING BULLIED?

Even if your child does not complain about being mistreated in school, there are some physical signs which should put you on the alert: stomach aches or headaches, difficulties breathing, severe bouts of eczema, nausea, vomiting, and so on. If you notice any of these clues, see if they have any physical marks on their body: scratches, bruises, marks left by blows, and so on. Finally, you may notice changes in their behaviour: they may shut themselves in their room more and more often, no longer work in class or withdraw into themselves.

If you spot any of these signs, be vigilant and do not be afraid to talk to them about it and then act, but always make sure that you have their consent and support. You should always have their best interests at heart.

WHAT SHOULD I DO IF MY CHILD IS BEING BULLIED?

Even if you know that your child is being bullied, talking with the bully's parents is never the best solution. The conversation will very likely take an unpleasant turn, and your child could suffer as a result and their situation may get even worse. The best thing to do would therefore be to organise a meeting with the headteacher and the teaching staff in order to find a solution. You could also talk with the head education advisor. If need be, get someone from the Parent Council to go with you.

If, in spite of your best efforts, the bullying continues, it might be necessary to make a complaint in order to resolve the situation.

SHOULD I MAKE MY CHILD MOVE SCHOOL TO SPARE THEM FURTHER PAIN?

You should only consider changing schools as a last resort. If you move your child to a different school straight away, this could:

- give the bully the impression that their actions have no consequences, which might encourage them to turn on other students;
- confirm your child as a victim who is incapable of adapting or integrating, which is a label that will become more and more difficult to break out of.

However, if both of your efforts do nothing to change the situation, it will eventually be necessary to move your child to another school. It is important to work on both their self-confidence and their trust in you, particularly by encouraging open conversation, in order to minimise their trauma, allow them to find a degree of calm in their life and help them to thrive at school.

WHAT SHOULD I DO IF MY CHILD IS THE ONE WHO IS DOING THE BULLYING?

If you notice that your child targets one of their classmates on a daily basis, you should talk with them to understand why they have taken on this role, so they will then be able to let it go. You will obviously not be alone in this task: help is available not only from the teachers in the school, but also – if the situation requires it – from a specialist who will be able to support and advise you.

AS A TEACHER, HOW CAN I BRING UP BULLYING IN CLASS?

If you want to teach a class about bullying, it is important to make the lesson interactive and give everyone the chance to express their opinion.

Firstly, you need to define the concept and the devastating effects of bullying on the victim. Do not be afraid to ask willing students to explain this in their own words. You can then support their definition by showing videos or cartoons made by respected organisations to raise awareness among young people about this problem which affects the majority of schools. Alongside this, you can also suggest different activities to your students: writing workshops, drama classes, making posters, and so on. If they feel they can relate to the problem, you could also suggest that they do an anti-bullying project (posters, videos, campaigns, etc.) and take part in a competition (such as Actionwork's Anti-Bullying Week Competition).

We want to hear from you!
Leave a comment on your online library
and share your favourite books on social media!

FURTHER READING

BIBLIOGRAPHY

- Aymon, G. (2013) *Ma réputation*. Arles: Actes Sud Junior.
- Ben Kemoun, H. (2013) *La Fille seule dans le vestiaire des garçons*. Paris: Flammarion.
- Blaya, C. (2013) *Les ados dans le cyberespace. Prises de risque et cyberviolence*. Louvain-La-Neuve: De Boeck Supérieur.
- Couples et Familles. (2014) *Comment réagir face au harcèlement scolaire?* [Online]. [Accessed 31 May 2017]. Available from: <http://www.couplesfamilles.be/index.php?option=com_content&view=article&id=377:comment-reagir-face-au-harcelementscolaire-&catid=6:analyses-et-reflexions&Itemid=9>
- Debarbieux, É. (2011) Refuser l'oppression quotidienne : la prévention du harcèlement à l'école. Éducation.gouv.fr. [Online]. [Accessed 31 May 2017]. Available from: <http://www.education.gouv.fr/cid55897/refuser-l-oppressionquotidienne-la-prevention-du-harcelement-a-l-ecole-rapportd-eric-debarbieux.html>
- Dieu, A-M. (2013) *Harcèlement : tous concernés !*. [Online]. [Accessed 9 May 2016]. Available from: <https://www.laligue.be/leligueur/articles/harcelement-tous-concernes-!>
- Ditch the Label. (2016). *Annual Bullying Survey 2016 – Bullying Statistics in the UK*. [Online]. [Accessed 31 May 2017]. Available from: <https://www.ditchthelabel.org/annual-bullying-survey-2016/>
- Fraisse, N. (2015) *Stop au harcèlement !* Paris:

Calmann-Lévy.
* Infor.jeunes.eu. (No date) *Harcèlement : que dit la loi ?* [Online]. [Accessed 19 May 2016]. Available from: <http://inforjeunes.eu/harcelement-dit-loi/>
* Jimenes, G. (2011) *Harcèlement !* Paris: Oskar Éditions.
* Kantouris, M. (2004) *Ne te laisse pas faire, petit ours !* Paris: Mango jeunesse.
* Konnecke, O. (2003) *Le Grand Méchant Bill.* Brussels: L'École des loisirs.
* Larsen de Susin Nielsen, H. K. (2013) *Le Journal malgré lui.* Paris: Hélium Éditions.
* Piquet, E. (2014) *Te laisse pas faire ! Aider son enfant face au harcèlement à l'école.* Paris: Payot & Rivages.
* Romano, H. (2015) *Harcèlement en milieu scolaire.* Paris: Dunod.

ADDITIONAL SOURCES

* Lutango, M. N. (2015) *A handbook of SCHOOL BULLYING: Dealing with the problem of bullying at school.* CreateSpace Independent Publishing Platform.
* Olweus, D. (1993) *Bullying at School: What We Know and What We Can Do.* New Jersey: Wiley-Blackwell.

www.50minutes.com

Ebook EAN: 9782806299871

Paperback EAN: 9782808000550

Legal Deposit: D/2017/12603/455

Cover: © Primento

Digital conception by Primento, the digital partner of publishers.

Made in the USA
Monee, IL
07 July 2026

56550251R00020